THE

JOY

OF CHRISTMAS

THE

JOY

OF CHRISTMAS

JANE HUGHES PAULSON

STARK BOOKS
**Andrews McMeel
Publishing**
Kansas City

00 01 02 03 04 BIN 10 9 8 7 6 5 4 3 2 1

Library of Congress Cataloging-in-Publication Data
Paulson, Jane Hughes.
  The joy of Christmas / Jane Hughes Paulson.
      p. cm.
  ISBN 0-7407-1152-0 (pbk.)
    1. Christmas. I. Title.

GT4985 .P393 2000
394.2663—dc21   00-55714

Book design by Holly Camerlinck

For my not so tiny Tim, with love and thanks
for all our Christmases past, present, and future

INTRODUCTION

❄

Christmas has good associations for me. I have kept an Advent calendar for as long as I can remember. Ritually I open the little windows that count down the December days until the twenty-fifth. As a child I knew that Christmas meant my mother, a school administrator, would be off work. Then she baked cranberry nut bread and kept a lot of presents locked in the trunk of the car—the only place she was certain her four offspring could not penetrate.

We never bought our tree before Christmas Eve, a tradition I have abandoned. There was a specialness to waiting, my father told me. As an adult I became aware of the substantial savings it means as well. Our TV room was transformed by the arrival of the sturdy Scotch pine. We had bubble lights and favorite ornaments. Mine was a silver bird with a spun-glass tail. My red-felt-and-artificial-ermine-trimmed Christmas stocking materialized from the bottom of a box, and I knew that by dawn it would be filled with walnuts, oranges, and cherry chocolates, a shepherd's pipe, colored pencils, a gyroscope, and other holiday loot.

Christmas morning never disappointed. We four children lined up in the hall upstairs. Daddy went ahead to turn on the lights on the tree. Then, youngest first, we raced to the mantel hung with bulging stockings and beyond, where what seemed to me then a glorious gift world was spread at the base of our blinking tree.

I remember a few of the gifts: a Betsy McCall doll, a cook set with miniature Betty Crocker cake mixes, and especially a metal musical pie that played "Sing a Song of

Sixpence" as you wound a tiny crank at the side. When you got to "four and twenty blackbirds"—SPROING—five flat black plastic birds burst out of slits in the tin crust for the "baked in a pie" finale. Push them back in and you could do it all over again. I loved that pie!

What I remember most about Christmas is the sensory extravaganza! The aromas of my grandmother's Parker House rolls baking in the oven beside the turkey were blissful torture. We ate turkey only twice a year, Thanksgiving and Christmas, and I loved it. My parents didn't entertain often, so the preparations for Christmas dinner were novel. The sound of my mother ordering for tables to be moved and chairs to be gotten was thrilling. The sight of the dazzling dinner table laid with all the best appealed to my budding nest-building instincts.

My job was to peel mountains of potatoes. I didn't mind. My efforts at the kitchen sink, while I was staring out into the backyard of a Missouri winter, would result in a heavy bowl of steaming mashed potatoes, a picture-perfect cube of margarine melting at the center, a dusting of orange paprika outlining the whipped peaks.

I've been doing the Christmas dinner for our extended family for more than ten years. From the first I was determined to create fond memories and traditions for our three sons, who were a lot more interested in their G.I. Joes than in the pine swags on the stairs. My husband claimed my standards were too high, but he hadn't seen *Better Homes'* December issue!

It took a few years, but we found our middle ground, where Christmas became a time to come together, not a time to fall apart. I admit, lowering my expectations helped. I focused more on family. We lit an Advent wreath each evening at dinner. That addition to our routine helped remind us all of the spiritual heart of the season—because the real magic of the holidays is not that Christmas makes problems disappear but that it makes them visible. People want to help other people. Acts of charity and thoughtfulness, more smiles, more connectedness of neighbors and communities, that's magic!

Sometimes people grumble about the commercialization of Christmas, but I marvel that the celebration of the birth of Christ each year produces a palpable spirit of hope, good cheer, and generosity. A lot of people knock themselves out at Christmas primarily for the right reasons, making it the giving season. A season of love and a season of, by my count, at least five hundred joys.

THE

JOY

OF CHRISTMAS

Everywhere—everywhere, Christmas
    tonight!
Christmas in land of the fir tree and
    pine,
Christmas in lands of the palm tree and
    vine,
Christmas where snow peaks stand
    solemn and white,
Christmas where corn fields lie sunny
    and bright,
Everywhere, everywhere, Christmas
    tonight.

—Phillips Brooks

THE
JOY
OF CHRISTMAS

The first sighting of eggnog
in the grocery dairy case

❄

Driving around with the family
to see the neighborhood Christmas lights.
There always seems to be one house that's a
real standout. For me it was the place
with a near actual-size sleigh on the roof
and eight very lifelike reindeer in attendance,
all backlit. It was very impressive!

Midnight church services: There's something remarkable about going to church in the middle of the night.

Baby Jesus

Being home for Christmas, wherever that is for you. It might be the home where you grew up, or the home where you raised your family, or the place you've gathered to celebrate this year. Home.

A big, beautifully wrapped mystery package
with your name on it under the tree

❄

The Macy's parade

❄

Watching *It's a Wonderful Life* for the
umpteenth time

Waiting up on Christmas Eve
to catch a glimpse of Santa

❄

The North Pole

The North Pole became Santa's

place of residence in 1882.

The artist Thomas Nast, who created

Santa's present-day image,

put the address on the jolly old elf's

mailbox in a drawing for

Harper's Weekly. He's lived there

ever since!

Sleigh rides

❄

Leaving out cookies and milk for Santa:
Our family favorite is "snickerdoodles."
They're buttery rich with cinnamon
and sugar on top. Santa loves them!

❄

Red and green M&M's

Icicles hanging from the eaves

Strings of fresh cranberries
to weave on the tree

The holiday account at the bank that
you've been saving in all year

Santa's flying reindeer: Have an after–Christmas dinner contest to name them: Dasher, Dancer, Prancer, Vixen, Comet, Cupid, Donder, and Blitzen. Rudolph is probably the most famous but was not one of the original eight. The winner gets a goofy prize.

❄

Wooden soldier nutcrackers

A sprig of mistletoe hanging from the doorway

❄

Someone to kiss under the mistletoe

The mistletoe hung in the castle hall,

The holly branch shone on the old

   oak wall;

And the baron's retainers were blithe

   and gay,

And keeping their Christmas holiday.

—*Thomas Haynes Bayly*

A Christmas puppy with a cold, damp nose

❄

Red woolen mittens

Baby's first Christmas: Be sure to hang
a stocking for the little one, too!

Finding the perfect tree
for the right price

Being at your low weight
before the holidays

❄

Being really inspired by
the Christmas spirit and shoveling snow
for a neighbor or friend

Window-shopping to see
the Christmas decorations:
If you live in a city or near one,
go to the fanciest shopping street
and take a stroll through the
winter wonderland.

❄

Free gift wrapping

Christmas lists

❄

Paper-white narcissus blooming
from the bulbs you forced

*H*ow to force paper-white narcissus:
Get bulbs at any nursery or home and
garden center. Fill a pretty bowl with
marbles (or pebbles or sand). Cover the
bulbs only enough to anchor them. Add
water to just below the tops of the marbles.
Leave them in a cool place with partial light
until they root. Then move them into full
sun and keep them well watered. Once they
bloom, move them to partial sun. Enjoy!

THE
JOY
OF CHRISTMAS

Letters to Santa

❄

Christmas wreaths: traditional evergreen,
holly, laurel, whatever you like.
I recently saw a fabulous wreath
made of cranberries, and I love
the ones with wrapped candies and
a pair of scissors to help yourself.

Self-sticking Christmas gift tags

❄

The Christmas tree at
Rockefeller Center

THE
JOY
OF CHRISTMAS

An ornament exchange:
Have friends over for coffee and dessert.
Ask each to bring two ornaments
to exchange. Everyone will leave with
two new treasures.

❄

A basket of pinecones

Fuzzy earmuffs

❄

Christmas catalogs: I get a lot of good
gift ideas for guys from the ones
filled with gadgets: Sharper Image,
Brookstone, and Hammacher Schlemmer.
The gardening catalogs, Smith & Hawken
and Gardeners Eden, for example, are
great for inspired floral arrangements
and decorating with Christmas greenery.

The snow in moonlight

Ho, ho, ho!

At Christmas be merry

and thankful withal.

—*Washington Irving*

Mrs. Claus

❄

Christmas elves

Having Christmas tree–shaped
guest soap in the bathroom

On-line Christmas shopping:
Try connecting in the off-hours when
the Web site may not be so in demand.

Snow angels

❄

Gingerbread men with silver
candy buttons

Letting your kids decorate their own
tabletop tree with decorations they
make themselves

✼

A brightly colored stocking cap
that covers your ears

Tree-trimming parties

❄

Going to see a local production
of *The Nutcracker*

*T*chaikovsky's *Nutcracker* is probably the most frequently performed ballet. Loved by young and old, it has become a holiday tradition. Although it premiered in St. Petersburg in December 1892 to lukewarm reviews, it has survived to become a staple of many of the world's finest ballet companies.

THE

JOY

OF CHRISTMAS

A train on tracks around
the Christmas tree: Mine is just the
toy store "special offer," but it has
a locomotive that puffs real smoke!
I load the log car with candy canes.

❄

The Grinch

Small mesh bags of gold foil–wrapped
chocolate coins

❄

Taking canned and packaged food
to a food bank

❄

Warm boots

THE
JOY
OF CHRISTMAS

An Advent chain: Advent is a time of waiting and preparation. Try this with your kids. Cut several sheets of construction paper (or any paper) into strips. Each day in December, make a note of one thing you're grateful for on a strip. Read them aloud, if the kids want to. Then glue the ends of each strip to make a ring. Every day add a ring to form a paper chain. On Christmas Eve hang it on the tree.

Watching videos of past Christmases

❄

Buying Christmas Seals:
Help fight lung disease.

Baking Christmas cookies

Receiving Christmas cookies

Christmas won't be Christmas

without presents.

—*From* Little Women *by Louisa May Alcott*

Gingerbread houses

❄

The soloist hitting the high note
in "O Holy Night"

Coming downstairs on Christmas morning

❄

Remembering you own a
Christmas sweater in time to wear it

THE
JOY
OF CHRISTMAS

Watching Christmas cooking shows
on the Food Network—I'm a big
Sara Moulton fan. Her food is elegant
but homey, and she always gives you a lot
of encouragement. My oldest son loves
Emeril Lagasse and makes his
cocktail sauce for my Christmas shrimp
appetizer. It's a big hit!

❄

Leaving food for the birds on top
of the snow and watching them eat up

Extended hours at the post office

❄

Mincemeat pie with hard sauce

Jingle bells

❄

Yule logs

$\mathcal{L}$ighting the Yule log on Christmas Eve
has been a tradition for centuries in Europe
and has roots going back to the Vikings and
pre-Christian times. Lighting the log
symbolized the victory of light over
darkness, and the promise of good crops
and fertility. Today logs are decorated with
evergreens and pinecones and tied with
ribbon. In old England the log was
ceremoniously dragged through the feasting
hall to the fireplace before being lit.

THE
JOY
OF CHRISTMAS

Eating the cookies and milk
you left out for Santa

❄

A dad teaching his daughter
to ride her new bike on Christmas Day

Kissing Santa Claus in your living room

❄

Snowmen! When I was growing up,
ours always had carrot noses and
green olives stuffed with pimentos
for eyeballs!

Getting the Christmas ornaments
out of the garage, basement, closet, or attic

❄

Christmas trees tied to the tops of cars

Free delivery

❄

A Christmas cookie party: Bring some,
eat some, take some home.

Eating from someone's Christmas china

The idea of "Peace on Earth"

Come, bring with a noise,

My merrie, merrie boyes,

The Christmas Log to the firing;

While my good Dame, she

Bids ye all be free;

And drink to your hearts desiring.

—*Robert Herrick*

Breakfast with Santa

❄

Hearing reindeer on the roof
on Christmas Eve

Sugared fruit: plums, grapes,
pears, apples . . . pretty!

❄

Live nativities: There was one
in my neighborhood when I was
growing up. It had the cutest little
black lamb.

Cutting down your own Christmas tree

❄

Watching a theatrical production
of *A Christmas Carol*

A gift of Christmas treats on a
china plate for you to keep

❄

Getting a lot of Christmas cards,
especially ones with photos

Chimneys for Santa to come down

❄

A pot of poinsettias

$\mathcal{P}$oinsettias are native to Mexico,

where they were known as flame plants.

They were introduced to

the United States by Joel Poinsett

in 1828, while he served as ambassador

to Mexico, and were named for him.

Miniature Christmas villages
with lights in the windows and skaters
on the mirror lake

❄

Canned whipped cream

Building a fire in the fireplace hung
with Christmas stockings

❄

The "kids'" table

THE

JOY

OF CHRISTMAS

Volunteering at a soup kitchen
or food pantry

A living Christmas tree

Holiday tea parties: They don't have to
be a big deal. Last year I asked two good
friends over, made a plate of egg salad
sandwiches and a pot of tea, and put out a
few Christmas cookies. It was easy and fun.
My friends enjoyed it so much we've
continued to get together for tea at one
another's homes about once a month.
A lot of times I stop myself from doing
something because I think it will take too
much time. If I keep it simple,
I can make it happen.

The green bean casserole

Wild geese flying in formation
over your house

Marzipan

I heard the bells on Christmas Day

Their old, familiar carols play

And wild and sweet the word repeat

Of peace on earth, goodwill to men!

—*Henry Wadsworth Longfellow*

Keeping tapes or CDs of Christmas
favorites in the car and singing along:
One year a close friend compiled
a selection of traditional, classic,
and offbeat songs, by artists from
Handel to Mel Tormé, and gave it as a gift.
It was one of the best presents
I ever received.

❄

Baked country ham

Christmas tree skirts

❄

Getting what you asked for

❄

Pomanders

Hanging your favorite Christmas ornament on the tree: My current first choice is a flat brass cutout, shiny on one side, painted on the other with a rocking horse and three well-dressed Victorian boys riding wildly on its back. It reminds me of my three guys, though I never could have gotten them into those fancy clothes.

❄

Christmas specials on TV

A bowl of nuts

❄

A good nutcracker

❄

Holly

Holly was plentiful in northern Europe.

Its prickly leaves and brilliant red berries

reminded the early Christians there of

Christ's crown of thorns and the blood he

shed to redeem them. By some accounts it

was known as the holy tree, and it was used

to decorate homes and churches.

The smell of Christmas
dinner cooking

❄

Leftovers!

Deciding to donate that jar of change
on your dresser to a local charity

Putting your kids to bed
on Christmas Eve

Christmas crackers
on the dinner table

❄

Reading *The Polar Express*
by Chris Van Allsburg:
This is a must-have for a
Christmas book collection.

THE
JOY
OF CHRISTMAS

"Lite" eggnog

❄

Garlands of cedar and pine
on the mantel and stairs

Walking in the cold and smelling the
smoke from someone's chimney

❄

Bethlehem

For unto you is born this day in the
city of David, a Savior, which is
Christ the Lord.

—*Luke 2:11*

Asking a child what Santa wants

for Christmas

❄

Persimmon pudding

Discovering you carefully wound up
the strings of Christmas tree lights
when you packed them last year

✻

The salesclerk who says she thinks
they're all out but she'll check
in the back for you

Cinnamon, nutmeg, ginger, and cloves

❄

Putting out pictures
from other Christmases

A big stack of dry firewood piled up

near the house

❄

The three wise men:

Melchior, Gaspar, and Balthazar

Christmas tree lots

The nice people working in
Christmas tree lots who help get your tree
in the car

An estimated thirty-five million trees are destined to become the centerpieces of holiday decorating and celebrations in the United States. Christmas tree farmers renew their crops each year by planting one to three seedlings to replace each of those harvested.

Having film in your camera

on Christmas morning

❄

A mantel lined with lighted votive candles

THE

JOY

OF CHRISTMAS

Sleigh bells

❄

Being awakened by a child
on Christmas morning

Getting your picture taken with Santa:
It's not just for kids. The first year we
were married, my husband and I had
our picture taken with the man in red,
had copies made, and sent them
as Christmas cards.

❄

Twinkle lights

Coming in out of the cold
after Christmas shopping

❄

The smell of the Christmas tree
in your house: Balsam, Noble, Fraser
or Douglas fir, blue or white spruce,
Scotch or Virginia pine, pick your favorite.
They all smell wonderful!

Making a video
of Christmas festivities

❄

Remembering to factor in gift wrapping:
Don't leave it all till Christmas Eve.

At Christmas play and make good

cheer,

For Christmas comes but once a year.

—*Thomas Tusser in*

The Farmer's Daily Diet

Finding the right Christmas gift
at the last minute

❄

Buying pants that actually
fit your husband

THE
JOY
OF CHRISTMAS

Shining the silver and brass so it sparkles

❄

Ice skaters on a farm pond

Taking each of your children
on a Christmas outing, just the two of you:
Go window-shopping in the mall, have
a donut and cocoa in a cozy coffee shop.

❄

Bubble lights

Getting the tree to stand up in the
Christmas tree stand

❄

A Christmas apron

Kids' handmade ornaments

❄

A clear winter night sky filled with stars

Martin Luther is sometimes linked with adding lights to decorated Christmas trees. The story says he was walking in the woods on a winter night and saw the sky filled with stars. He was so moved he cut a small fir tree, went home, and decorated it with candles to signify the stars. In fact, the first written accounts of decorated Christmas trees didn't appear for another fifty years.

Snow globes

❄

Christmas fairies

THE
JOY
OF CHRISTMAS

Shiny brass fireplace tools

❄

Strands of tinsel: Don't be surprised
if you're still finding them under the
sofa at Easter.

Hearing carolers outside your
window or in the mall

❄

Velvet gift boxes

Trying to remember all the words to
"The Twelve Days of Christmas"

❄

Needlepoint pillows with
a holiday theme: candy canes, angels,
or a brass trumpet

An electric knife to carve the turkey

Someone who knows *how*

to carve the turkey

Heap on more wood!—the wind
　　is chill;
But let it whistle as it will,
We'll keep our Christmas merry still.

—*Sir Walter Scott*

A Christmas gift of absolutely sinful
chocolates

❄

A floral porcelain bowl filled with
tangerines. My favorite variety is satsuma—
tiny, sweet, and best of all, *seedless.*

Mulled wine

Putting an extra log on the fire

A Christmas toast with icy champagne
in a crystal flute

❄

Little toy soldiers

Hearing the guys talk about who's
going to win the Rose Bowl

Pomegranates

A garland of gumdrops

and licorice nibs

❆

Reading *The Night Before Christmas*

with your kids

$\mathcal{D}$r. Clement Clarke Moore was a professor of divinity in New York City and father of six. He also wrote poetry and on December 23, 1822, surprised his family by reading his *A Visit from Saint Nicholas.* A friend asked for a copy and had it printed anonymously the following year in the *Troy* [New York] *Sentinel.* It was reprinted many times in many papers before the serious-minded Moore, who thought the subject a bit frivolous, claimed authorship of what today is known as *The Night Before Christmas.*

A Christmas crown roast

Colored tissue paper

Mailing your Christmas cards so they'll
arrive before Christmas

Roasted chestnuts

Reading the story of Christmas from
the Bible—Luke 2:1–21.

❄

Place cards at the dinner table

Making cookie-dough ornaments
with the kids

A blooming Christmas cactus

My husband saying, "Bah! Humbug!"
but only half-meaning it

Finding a stash of Christmas presents
under the bed

Little Jack Horner

Sat in a corner

Eating his Christmas Pie;

He put in his thumb,

And pulled out a plum,

And said, "What a good boy am I!"

—*Anonymous*

Displaying your Christmas cards

✳

Old-fashioned oatmeal with brown sugar,
raisins, and a dash of cream.

Silly stocking stuffers: Once my husband
gave me a flashy "faux" diamond ring.
My dinner guests were dazzled.

A big dog wearing a jaunty red bow

Taking time to contemplate the
spiritual significance of the season

❄

Giving to Toys for Tots

A junior-sized Christmas tree
for the den or kids' room

❄

A gift tag reading
"Do Not Open Until Christmas"

Short, upbeat Christmas letters

❆

The Christmas tree lighting
at the White House

$\mathcal{P}$resident Calvin Coolidge

began the custom of having a large,

beautifully decorated and lighted tree

on the lawn of the White House

in 1923.

Going to the "Christmas dance"

❄

Christmas stamps

Getting a Christmas card from a
long-lost friend

❄

A mantel festooned with pine boughs
and silver balls

Rocking around the Christmas tree

Spiced cider with a

cinnamon swizzle stick

The Christmas angels

❄

Going for a walk after Christmas dinner:
If it's over forty degrees,
make it a long one!

Decorated gaslights

❄

Snow forts with hefty stockpiles
of snowballs

And blessed is the Christmas time

With music such as rang

A glorious strain o'er Bethlehem's

 plain

When angel voices sang.

—Lalia Mitchell

Guys who wear Santa Claus hats
around the office

❄

Being able to put something extra
in the mail carrier's and
newspaper deliverer's envelope

Steamed Christmas pudding: Douse it with brandy and set it aflame! That's a showstopper!

A wreath on the front grille of an SUV

Letting go at a sing-along of
Handel's *Messiah*

❄

Big Christmas gift bags for
odd-sized gifts

The bell-ringing Santas at the
Salvation Army stands

❄

Good friends who like to talk about
the future and laugh about the past

Getting the words to a bunch of
Christmas carols off the Internet

❄

Fruitcake

$\mathcal{D}$espite all the fruitcake jokes,

the Collins Street Bakery in Corsicana,

Texas, takes it seriously.

They sell over 1.5 million

in a single holiday season.

Someone must like it!

Using family photos to deck the halls

❄

Teddy bears

❄

Decorating the tree

Snow glistening

❄

Feeling connected, a sense
of community

❄

Christmas stencils in windows:
Remember Glass Wax?

Spending too much money on the
perfect gift for your mother:
One year we four grown kids
pooled resources and gave Mom a trip
to sunny Spain.

CHRISTMAS PUNCH:

I use a recipe from an ad for Cointreau.
Put a block of ice in a punch bowl,
add a bottle of Cointreau (¾ quart),
a fifth of vodka, I (6-ounce) can each
orange and pineapple juice concentrate,
and 3 quarts club soda, and stir.
Garnish with orange slices (decorated with
a few cranberries each studded by
a clove—optional). Makes 5 quarts
or 40 punch cups.

Putting your feet up after
Christmas shopping

❄

Flocking

Christmas is coming, the goose

    is getting fat,

Please put a penny in the

    old man's hat.

If you haven't got a penny,

    a ha'penny will do,

If you haven't got a ha'penny,

    God bless you!

—*Anonymous*

Dear Abby's annual Christmas
message to her readers

A new doll: My favorite doll was handmade
by my aunt. I got her when I was on the
brink of outgrowing dolls. She had a cherub
face with brown-felt crescent eyes and an
embroidered nose and smile. She came with
several outfits and prolonged my childhood,
I'm certain. I did outgrow my other dolls,
but I still have Sophie.

THE
JOY
OF CHRISTMAS

Christmas music in elevators

❄

Random acts of Christmas kindness

A slice of warm cranberry bread
with butter

✳

Taking a bubble bath by
Christmas-scented candlelight

French wired ribbon

❄

Angel wings

Reading *A Christmas Carol* out loud one
chapter a night leading up to Christmas Eve

❄

Candy canes: I'm not sure why,
but Christmas is the only time of year
I like them.

Accounts of Christmas candy shaped like a shepherd's crook appear as early as 1670 in Germany. Today's red-striped version is said to have religious origins as well. The white candy symbolized purity, and the red stripes, three narrow and one wide, represented the blood of Christ.

Getting grandparents to talk about their memories of Christmas when they were children

❄

A Christmas pin to wear on your winter coat: Snowmen, holly—I have one that looks like a Christmas tree lightbulb.

Really rich Scotch shortbread

❄

The ghosts of Christmas Past, Present,
and Future

The Christmas pickle ornament: A German tradition says to hide the pickle on the tree Christmas Eve. Whoever finds it gets a prize. If you don't have a pickle ornament, substitute. Kids get really excited about this ritual despite the packages under the tree.

❆

Snow on the mountains

A steaming cup of good coffee to sip
during the early-morning present opening

A cold wind turning your nose red

Not getting the "bug"
that's going around

❄

Mangers

And she brought forth her
firstborn son, and wrapped him
in swaddling clothes, and laid him
in a manger; because there was
no room for them in the inn.

—*Luke* 2:7

Starting a family Christmas tradition

❄

Keeping a family Christmas tradition:
Each year I give our boys an ornament.
They'll have a nice start on a collection
when they have trees of their own.

THE
JOY
OF CHRISTMAS

The big Hollywood studio
Christmas movie releases

❄

Christmas trifle in a glass pedestal bowl

Places where you can paint your own
pottery: Make your own Christmas
heirlooms! Platters are good.

❄

Getting time off

A turkey sandwich Christmas night
after everyone else has gone to bed—
with extra mayo, yum!

A silk Christmas scarf to
wear around your neck

Glitter

❄

Homemade chocolate truffles

No-Trouble Truffles:

1 cup heavy cream

2 (10-ounce) packages semisweet chocolate bits

2 tablespoons unsweetened cocoa

¼ cup chopped pecans or pistachios

Bring cream nearly to a boil over medium heat. Stir in chocolate pieces until smooth. Pour mixture into a 9-by-13-inch baking dish; cover and refrigerate until firm.

Using a spoon, scoop up small amounts of

the mixture and shape into balls with your

hands. Work fast. Rechill if the mixture

softens too much. Roll half in chopped nuts

and half in unsweetened cocoa. Refrigerate

until ready to serve. Makes 4 dozen.

Advent calendars

Christmas guest towels in the powder room

A new outfit for Christmas Day

Making a Christmas wish come true

Office Christmas parties: If spouses
of employees are invited, make an effort
to include them in conversations.
If alcohol is served, drink moderately.

❄

Watching *The Bishop's Wife*—Cary Grant
as an angel, that's heaven!

Hearing bells on Christmas morning

❄

Gold, frankincense, and myrrh

A church decorated for Christmas services

❄

Making it a goal to lower your stress level:
Try breaking the holidays into small
assignments. Sit down with a calendar at
the beginning of December and give
yourself one or two things to do a day.
I've learned to delegate (my husband gets
the tree and puts on the lights). I've also
learned not to be a perfectionist.
The tree and lights always look great!

From our snug fireside this

Christmastide

We'll keep old Winter out.

—*Thomas Noel*

A Rice Krispies Treats house—easier to make and assemble, and, for me, tastier than the gingerbread counterpart

❄

Lots of real whipped cream

Being able to stick to your budget
and not feel like Scrooge

❄

Fancy holiday collections of
perfumes and bath items

Swedish glogg: This aromatic drink is made with red and port wines, simmered with spices (cinnamon, cardamom, and cloves), and served warm with a sprinkling of orange zest and toasted almonds.

A Christmas memory book: After dinner pass around a special binder or notebook. Ask your family to write a few lines each about what is special for them about this year's Christmas. Put the notebook away with your ornaments after Christmas, and do it again next year.

A tray of lighted candle pillars
glowing warmly

Snow blowers

A Christmas quilt: Star of Bethlehem,
Pine Tree, or Pointed Star to mention a few

❄

Putting out your nativity set

St. Francis of Assisi popularized

nativity scenes. In 1223 in the

Italian village of Greccio

he re-created the Bethlehem stable

complete with live animals.

A special breakfast Christmas morning:
My mother always sends us Wolferman's
English muffins for Christmas. Wolferman's
was a family grocery and bakery in Kansas
City, where I grew up. The stores are gone,
but they still make their muffins, jams, and
a few other things available in their catalog.
We have them toasted, dripping with
cinnamon butter (soft butter mixed with
sugar and cinnamon to taste). There's
also hot chocolate, or my favorite,
strong English tea.

A Christmas watch with a
cheery red band

Falling snow

Christmas stickers

Cyber Santa: Go ahead, decorate a
virtual tree with virtual ornaments!

❄

Hanging a wreath inside the house

Laughter

Sending Christmas cards

Not sending Christmas cards

❄

"Silent Night" sung by a children's choir
in any language—I'm partial to the
French "Sainte Nuit." My high school
glee club used to carol in our local
shopping district. When we sang it, you
could hear a pin drop—even in the snow.

Let sinned against, and sinning

Forget their strife's beginning,

And join in friendship now:

Be links no longer broken,

Be sweet forgiveness spoken,

Under the Holly bough.

—*Charles Mackay*

Artificial trees with prestrung lights—
for the time-challenged

❄️

Shimmery nail polish: You can look like
a party even when driving the car pool.

Decking the halls

❄

My sister Michele's hot buttered rum

Sharing Christmas long distance with
a special call to someone far away

❄

That Santa fits down all those chimneys!

A child's smile when she opens your gift

Doing something special for an
elderly neighbor: Drop off a poinsettia
and stay to visit for more than a minute,
offer to take her on an errand,
or run an errand for him.

Remembering it is better to give
than to receive

❄

Roast Christmas turkey

The turkey was introduced to

Europeans in the sixteenth century

by merchants from the Levant,

which included Turkey. The fowl is

alleged to have been named after

the country and became the bird of choice

at Christmas feasts.

Letting yourself off the "guilt" hook
and enjoying Christmas

❄

Glena's Christmas snowball surprise:
Roll ice cream balls in coconut and
drizzle with hot fudge.

THE

JOY

OF CHRISTMAS

A Christmas floral arrangement
for your table sent ahead by a
thoughtful dinner guest

❄

Giant-sized rolls of gift wrap

Being able to make a Christmas basket
for the needy

❄

Tasting falling snowflakes

An excuse to wear a bunch of those
crystal-beaded bracelets and shiny bangles

❄

A Christmas bonus!

Refusing a few of the holiday
invitations and spending the time
with your family

❄

A Christmas birthday

There's a dear old tree, an evergreen
tree,
And it blossoms once a year.
'Tis loaded with fruit from top to root,
And it brings to all good cheer.
For its blossoms bright are small
candles white
And its fruit is dolls and toys.
And they all are free for both you
and me
If we're good little girls and boys.

—*Luella Wilson Smith, from*
St. Nicholas *magazine*

Ready-to-serve holiday party platters from the grocery store

✻

Shopping mall Santas: The first Christmas I lived in Los Angeles, I took my sons with me to Little Tokyo. There we discovered "Shogun" Santa. A dynamic-looking samurai sat inside a small pagoda on a throne. He wore the traditional helmet and had a giant sword. When he asked the boys if they'd been good, they really took him seriously! We got a great picture that year!

Shopping early

❄

Watching birds celebrate at the tree
you made for them tied with strings
of cereal and seeds

A good reason to wear
something spangly

❄

Colored plastic wrap

Despite what you've heard, poinsettias are not toxic plants. Sparky's gonna make it!

❄

A big gift box of Christmas citrus: fragrant grapefruits and oranges

Answering machines! Grab that
pre-Christmas catnap.

❄

The posada

Posada is Spanish for "shelter." In Mexico an important tradition is the posada party, reenacting Mary and Joseph's search for shelter in Bethlehem. For nine nights, from December 16 through 24, families celebrate, taking the part of pilgrims and innkeepers. They gather with candles and song outside the home of the host. Half the group goes inside, and the other half asks for shelter. Soon everyone is welcomed inside, and the party (usually featuring a piñata) begins. The biggest party is on Christmas Eve, often followed by midnight Mass.

Going to a religious service that is
geared especially for kids

❄

Christmas tartans

Remembering less is more

Snow clouds threatening on the horizon

Arranging for a phone call from Santa:
See a kid's face light up when you tell him
who's on the line.

❄

Christmas place mats for the table,
especially the homemade variety

Holiday dinner guests who offer to bring something: I always gratefully say yes!

❄

Sharing your favorite holiday memories with your friends and children: One of mine is of the day after Christmas. I sneaked off to the bedroom to lie down. The three boys found me, and while I tried to nap they put together an elaborate dollhouse, complete with furnishings, that I had been given. I lay there smiling, listening to my young sons discuss the directions and negotiate the placement of flowerpots and baby buggies. It was great! The thing would probably still be in the box if it weren't for them!

Being filled with goodwill and cheer
by volunteering at a hospital

❅

Falling in love with Christmas
all over again

Blessed is the season

which engages the whole world

in a conspiracy of love.

—*Hamilton Wright Mabie*

Taking the kids to buy an extra gift
and giving it to a local charity

Being snowbound!

Homemade Christmas biscotti—
heaven with a cup of tea

❄

Royal icing

Finding a terrific tray, scarf, or pin
that will suit several people on your list
and buying a bunch

Sledding downhill on your stomach

THE

JOY

OF CHRISTMAS

Christmas pageants

❄

Offering a blessing before Christmas dinner

Holding hands while you offer the
blessing before Christmas dinner

❄

Caroling around the neighborhood
with your friends

The word *carol* comes from the Greek word *choraulein* (*chorus,* "the dance," and *aulein,* "to play the flute"). Originally it referred to a dance, particularly a ring dance accompanied by music. The word eventually came to mean only the dance music. Words to the music were added around the fifteenth century, and they were performed at religious festivals.

Snowdrifts

❄

Simple directions to assemble the new bike

❄

A friend who offers to assemble the
new bike for you

Getting out all the "good stuff" to set
the Christmas dinner table

✻

The trunks of palm trees
wrapped with small white lights—
Christmas California style

UNICEF Christmas cards,
a good deed made easy: The proceeds go
to meeting health and education needs
of kids around the world.

Doing your nails a Christmas red:
My husband has discovered nail polish
makes a good stocking stuffer, too.

THE
JOY
OF CHRISTMAS

Being naughty

Being nice

Learning to say Merry Christmas
in other languages—*Feliz Navidad,*
Joyeux Noël, Buon Natale!

Yes, Virginia, there is a Santa Claus.

—*Francis P. Church, editorial page,*

New York Sun

THE

JOY

OF CHRISTMAS

Virginia O'Hanlon: The eight-year-old
asked her father about the existence
of Santa Claus. He answered,
"If you see it in the *Sun*, it's so."
(see page 205)

Gifts from the heart

A Christmas photo album

Little boys with scrubbed faces, clean white
shirts, and red bow ties

❄

Taking Christmas dinner to a friend
recovering from an operation

❄

Christmas boxers

Finding a perfect gift for your child's favorite teacher: My boys often have insights I don't. My middle son surprised me when he was in third grade by saying he already had a gift for his teacher. He was especially fond of this woman; we all were. I asked him what he was giving her. He went to the kitchen cupboard and took out a Santa mug with his name painted around the top. He loved the mug, and I reminded him that it was his. "I know," he said, "but I want her to have it." I helped him wrap it. The teacher later told me it was one of the best gifts she ever received.

A bunch of Christmas roses that look
smashing in that silver sugar bowl you've
never used

❆

Christmas cashmere: How about an elegant
red pashmina stole to wrap yourself in?

❆

Rudolph the red-nosed reindeer

$\mathcal{G}$ene Autry recorded the musical version

of "Rudolph the Red-Nosed Reindeer"

in 1949, but the original story was

a product of Montgomery Ward and Co.

Robert May, a copywriter, and

Denver Gillis, an illustrator and

fellow employee, were drafted into service

to create the annual Christmas coloring

book. The result was Rudolph. The store

distributed 2.4 million copies in 1939.

Making a gift for Granddad with the kids:
Paperweights are easy. We found a
smooth, rounded stone and painted it.
My son was proud of the finished product,
and so was his grandfather.

❄

Reading O. Henry's
"The Gift of the Magi"

Saint Nicholas

❄

Finally putting an organ donor sticker
on your license, ready to give the
most precious gift, life

A Christmas getaway: Pick a pineapple
Christmas morning in Hawaii!

Christmas socks: My favorite pair is
red with green Christmas trees. There are
a lot of fun patterns for guys, too.
Coincidentally, these make great
stocking stuffers!

Grabbing the last "hot" toy of

the season on the shelf

❄

Gift certificates

Stolen moments with your special someone

in the midst of Christmas chaos

❄

A Christmas wedding

God rest you merry, gentlemen,

Let nothing you dismay;

Remember Christ our Savior,

Was born on Christmas Day.

—*Christmas carol*

My aunt Mitzi's frosted
cinnamon Christmas ring with
red and green maraschino cherries on top

❄

The guys all playing the new
video game after dinner

❄

Giant-sized garbage bags

Snow plows

❄

Hot cocoa with marshmallows in
a Christmas mug: My boys like the instant
varieties, but I love to make cocoa from
"scratch": hot milk, cocoa powder, a little
sugar, and vanilla. It takes an extra minute,
and there is the dirty pan, but when it
comes to cocoa, I'm worth it.

Taking advantage of the spirit of
the holiday to resolve some conflicts
with friends or family

❄

A blooming amaryllis

❄

A chance to use that beaded evening bag

An unexpected thank-you note
for your Christmas gift

Believing in Santa Claus

A Santa Claus Association

was founded in New York in 1914.

Its mission statement read,

"To preserve children's faith in Santa Claus."

The association also answered letters

to Santa.

Oil drum fires for skaters to warm
their hands and frozen toes

❄

The little drummer boy: My mother
loved the song, and I loved the image
of the little boy playing his drum
for the holy family in the stable.

A post–Christmas dinner game
of Scrabble or Monopoly

Frost on the windows

A Christmas baby

Getting your Cub Scout troop to make
get-well cards and delivering them
at the hospital

Luminarias

Holiday magic, feel it in the air!

Old-fashioned reindeer sweaters

❄

Christmas-scented potpourris

The whole world is a Christmas tree,

And stars its many candles be.

—*Harriet Blodgett*

Advent wreaths

❄

Setting a lovely Christmas dinner table

❄

Not getting lumps of coal
in your Christmas stocking

THE
JOY
OF CHRISTMAS

Spending more time with your kids:
Give them what they *really* want
for Christmas.

❄

Shepherds watching their flocks
on Christmas night

❄

The wagging tail when you give
your dog that nylon bone he's
been hankering for

❄

Making a wish on the Christmas star

❄

Idie's Christmas meringues

❄

Nesting doll Santas

❄

Jack Frost

THE

JOY

OF CHRISTMAS

$\mathcal{J}$ack Frost, the sprite responsible for

nipping at your nose with winter cold,

probably originated in Scandinavia.

Norse myths refer to the wind god

who had a son named Frosti,

which means "frost."

Stores closing early on Christmas Eve:
Whew! Ready or not, you've got to stop.

Reading the story of the birth of Jesus
with your family and talking about
the spiritual significance of the holiday

THE
JOY
OF CHRISTMAS

An heirloom gift: an antique handkerchief,
piece of silver, or tablecloth . . . priceless

❄

Pannetone: traditional Italian Christmas
cake—golden, light, and studded
with candied fruits and pine nuts

Little girls in white tights
and velvet dresses

❄

Giving in to the urge to bake
banana bread for the neighbors

❄

Peanut brittle

Getting out of snow-sodden things
and into something warm

Fur muffs

Christopher Radko ornaments

When it's Christmas man is bigger

And is better in his part;

He is keener for the service that is

Prompted by his heart.

—*Edgar A. Guest*

Christmas cookie cutters

❄

Christmas cookbooks: I enjoy Susan Branch's *Christmas from the Heart of the Home* any time of year. Her writing is so friendly, and her illustrations are clever, even sweet, but not cloying. She includes a lot of personal stories about how she got a particular recipe and how she uses it when she entertains. Her "Mrs. McGurgler's Heavenly Waffles" are a Sunday morning standard at my house, and I often make her "Chocolate Pots de Cremes." This woman really loves Christmas and makes you feel good about loving it, too—even in July!

Secret Santas

❄

A cushion filled with fragrant
pine needles

❄

A Victorian feather tree

Christmas tree recycling programs: Call your local public works office and find out how to give your tree back to the environment.

❄

Losing the idea that your home has to be a perfect "Christmas wonderland"

❄

Remembering to talk more than eat at the Christmas parties

❄

The Christmas tree topper: star or angel

❄

Spicy pecans: The best I've ever had
were made with Smith's pecans from
Raymond, Mississippi. It's not too
cold there, but these pecans will
warm things up wherever you serve them!

$\mathcal{M}$Y FAVORITE SPICY PECANS:

1 pound pecan halves

3 tablespoons butter

3 tablespoons Worcestershire sauce

1 teaspoon salt

$\frac{1}{4}$ teaspoon cayenne pepper

$\frac{1}{2}$ teaspoon cinnamon

2 dashes of Tabasco

Melt butter and stir in all ingredients.

Add pecans and stir to coat. Spread pecans

on a baking sheet and roast (turning often)

at 300 degrees for about 30 minutes.

Cool and serve or store in airtight

containers. These make nice hostess gifts.

Christmas tights printed with
candy canes or holly

Learning the origins of a
Christmas tradition—the wreath,
the tree—and sharing it
with your family

Ribbon candy

Dropping everything to go play
in the snow

Buying a lot of extra batteries
in various sizes

❄

Comice pears, creamy and delicious
cousins to the Royal Rivieras and
Mavericks—'Tis their season!
No wonder the partridge was sitting
in a pear tree.

Spending more time *doing* holiday things
than preparing for them

❄

Cookie presses: Stamp Christmas
designs into sugar cookies

Going to a formal Christmas party
with my husband: If men only knew
how great they look in tuxedos!

❄

Knowing someone is wrapping a present
for you behind a locked door

Some say that ever 'gainst that
season comes,
Wherein our Saviour's birth is
celebrated,
The bird of dawning singeth all night
long;
And then, they say, no spirit can
walk abroad;
The nights are wholesome; then no
planets strike,
No fairy takes, nor witch hath power
to charm;
So hallow'd and so gracious is the
time

—Hamlet, *Act I, Scene 1*

Christmas sparkle: Pick up a few
crystal-trimmed headbands, barrettes,
or bobby pins and wear them.
These make great stocking stuffers, too!

❄

Spending time with someone
from another country learning
their Christmas traditions

UPS and Federal Express

The anticipation of a new doll
or bike in a child's eyes

Going to a museum and looking
at paintings of nativities: You can go
on-line and visit the world's greatest
museums from your den!

❄

Wearing red

❄

Ice skaters at Rockefeller Center

Hearing snow crunching as you
walk through it

❄

Buying ornaments half price on
Christmas Eve: Buy some for yourself
to replenish your supply. Buy extras
for hostess gifts and stocking stuffers.

F. W. Woolworth is credited

with commercializing Christmas in 1880

by reluctantly investing in

twenty-five dollars' worth of

German handblown ornaments.

They sold out in two days. Two years

later his order was for over

two hundred thousand pieces.

Being the designated driver:
Don't be a holiday statistic.

The Neapolitan Christmas tree
at the Metropolitan Museum in
New York City

The growing Christmas tree in
The Nutcracker

The Christmas house mouse,
the one who wasn't stirring

Taking time for some personal
reflection—the good and not so good
from the past year

Seeing a production of
Amahl and the Night Visitors

❄

Decorated trees: A travel account
dated 1605 reports a custom in
Strassburg of adding paper roses,
apples, and cookies to the tree.
The Pennsylvania Germans brought
the custom to America.

Wearing your favorite plaid flannel shirt

to wrap presents

❄

More laughter!

❄

Remembering that the words
Christmas and *mall* aren't synonymous

THE

JOY

OF CHRISTMAS

I will honor Christmas in my heart,

and try to keep it all the year.

—*Charles Dickens*

The Mexican Yule tree,
candle tree of life

❄

A glass jar lined antipasto style
with Christmas candy

Making Christmas merrier than ever
with a new activity, game, or special dish

A Christmas candle carousel:
a decoration from Denmark

Listening to medieval Christmas music
on the radio: It can be a soothing
change from the standard holiday fare.

❄

A great reason to wear that
silver-sequined tube top!

Putting out all the Christmas books you have: Start a collection if you don't have one. You can add to it each year. For me the "must-haves" include at least one retelling of the birth of Christ. It's easy to find an inexpensive copy of *The Night Before Christmas.* We also found regional versions, *The Cajun Night Before Christmas,* for example, where Santa arrives on a skiff pulled by eight alligators!

How the Grinch Stole Christmas and *The Snowman* were read year-round. There are so many! My favorite is *The Christmas Alphabet* by Robert Sabuda. Each letter is a Christmas icon pop-up. *G* is for *gift.* Lift the flap, up pops a tiny gift box for you to open, and there's a surprise inside. It's terrific. Kids and grown-ups both enjoy it. It makes a great gift itself.

A chandelier hung with
Christmas ornaments

A Christmas kitten

St. Lucia Day (December 13):
We have Sweden to thank for this
tradition of young girls in white
wearing crowns of lighted candles.

*S*t. Lucia was a Christian martyr in the fourth century in Sicily. How her fame spread to Sweden is not exactly clear, but she is revered there as the virgin saint, the bringer of light into the winter darkness. Originally it was a family tradition for the oldest daughter to wear a crown of lighted candles and carry a tray of coffee and saffron buns to her parents. Today her feast day is celebrated in various forms all over Sweden and in Swedish communities around the world.

THE

JOY

OF CHRISTMAS

Putting out a Christmas doormat

Christmas ties

Men who wear Christmas ties:
For fun, treat your husband or boss
to a new one now and then. Can a man
have too many Christmas ties?

❄

Taking your favorite low-calorie main
course to the Christmas buffet and eating it
instead of filling up on other
high-cal offerings

A holiday boat parade: In coastal cities and towns, private boats get decked out and cruise through the marina. It's a fun family activity.

❄

Remembering to smile a lot—people will smile back.

The candle in the window tradition:
Originally this was attributed to the Irish.
Now the candles are electric, but it's
pleasant to see the orangy flames at all the
windows of the house on a winter night.

❄

Putting a gift for yourself under the tree—
be sure to wrap it.

Filling a tall glass vase with
Christmas ornaments

❄

Re-gifting: Recycle the gifts you'll
never use or have three of and can't
take back. Who'll know?

The holly in the windy hedge

And round the Manor House the yew

Will soon be stripped to deck the

   ledge,

The altar, font and arch and pew,

So that the villagers can say

The church looks nice on Christmas

   Day.

—*Sir John Betjeman*

The Christmas stocking your mother
made you to hang from the mantel:
I decided to needlepoint a stocking for
my firstborn. He was an impatient six
by the time it was finished, but I did it!

❄

Shopping in an ethnic neighborhood:
Visit your local Chinatown
or Little Italy.

Glamming it up for a Christmas party

❄

Santa's overflowing bag of toys

THE

JOY

OF CHRISTMAS

Saving your Christmas cards to cut up
and reuse as gift tags next Christmas:
A hole punch and thin ribbon are all
you need. It's a good kid project.

❄

Golden brown stuffed Christmas goose

A two-thousand-piece dollhouse
that isn't missing a piece

❄

Places that let you defer payment
until March

Holiday Barbie

Wassail

Wassail is a drink the originated

in England. The name comes from

the Saxon toast *Was haile!* (Be healthy).

The fragrant drink was made of ale,

apples, and spices. It was sweetened

with sugar and served in a bowl.

Singing Christmas carols around the piano

❄

Someone who can play the piano

❄

Getting your gift orders in on time to avoid
more expensive shipping costs

Christmas coupons: For special things
you can't buy in the stores, like a trip to
a video arcade with Dad, or a visit to the
zoo with Mom, there are coupons.
Write them out on strips of paper
and use them as stocking stuffers, or
tie them to the tree. Kids love these and
like to make their own for parents
and siblings (for instance, "Good for
one loading of the dishwasher after dinner,
no complaints").

THE
JOY
OF CHRISTMAS

Holiday window boxes

❄

Snow days!

Christmas ivy topiaries tied with
plaid ribbon

❄

A new box of good stationery
to write thank-you notes

Christmas, Florida: They may not get snow at Christmas, but they get bundles of Christmas cards from all over the country wanting *that* postmark!

❄

New flannel pajamas in a holiday pattern: snowflakes or stars

Then the Grinch thought of

    something

he hadn't before! "Maybe

    Christmas,"

he thought, "doesn't come from a

    store."

—*Dr. Seuss (Theodor Seuss Geisel)*

Christmas concerts

Going with a friend of a different religion
to a holiday service for that faith

Giving your houseguests their own
Christmas stockings as gifts when
they arrive: They can hang them
Christmas Eve and feel a real part of
the family. Fill them with lots of little
wrapped goodies, so they will be
well occupied Christmas morning.

❄

A nap on the couch after
Christmas dinner

Collecting crèches

❄

Printing out "The Twelve Days
of Christmas" to sing after dinner

Candied orange peel

❄

Themed Christmas trees: the seaside,

teddy bears, you name it!

Lots of help with the
Christmas dinner dishes

❄

Bing Crosby singing
"White Christmas"

"*White Christmas*" by Irving Berlin

is reputed to be the most recorded

holiday song, with more than

five hundred versions in dozens

of languages.

A new jigsaw puzzle to work on
after Christmas dinner

A gift of homemade blackberry jam

Putting a moratorium on the
"nonpersonal" until after the
holidays—most things can wait.

❄

Not cooking dinner on Christmas Eve:
Go out for Chinese, or to a pancake house.
Get deli from the grocery store and eat
on paper plates by the fireplace if you've
got one, but don't cook.

Eggnog lattes

Watching *Miracle on 34th Street* in bed
with your kids

Music boxes that play "The First Noel"

Looking outside to see a stretch
of untrampled snow

THE

JOY

OF CHRISTMAS

A full Christmas stocking

A full heart